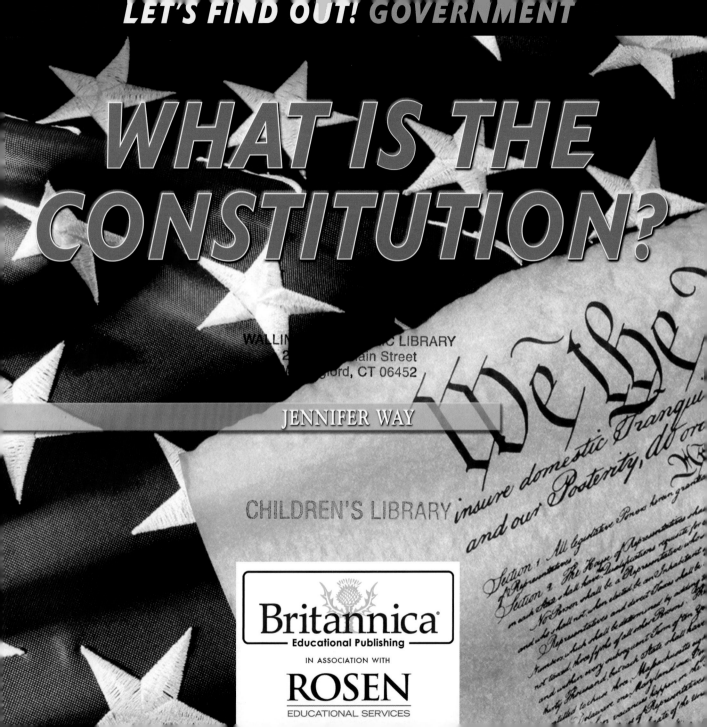

WHAT IS THE CONSTITUTION?

JENNIFER WAY

Britannica®
Educational Publishing

IN ASSOCIATION WITH

ROSEN
EDUCATIONAL SERVICES

Published in 2016 by Britannica Educational Publishing (a trademark of Encyclopædia Britannica, Inc.) in association with The Rosen Publishing Group, Inc.
29 East 21st Street, New York, NY 10010

Distributed exclusively by Rosen Publishing.
To see additional Britannica Educational Publishing titles, go to rosenpublishing.com.

First Edition

<u>Britannica Educational Publishing</u>
J.E. Luebering: Director, Core Reference Group
Mary Rose McCudden: Editor, Britannica Student Encyclopedia

<u>Rosen Publishing</u>
Hope Lourie Killcoyne: Executive Editor
Nelson Sá: Art Director
Danijah Brevard and Brian Garvey: Designers
Cindy Reiman: Photography Manager

Library of Congress Cataloging-in-Publication Data

Way, Jennifer, author.
What is the constitution?/Jennifer Way. — First edition.
        pages cm. — (Let's find out! Government)
Includes bibliographical references and index.
ISBN 978-1-62275-971-2 (library bound) — ISBN 978-1-62275-972-9 (pbk.) —
ISBN 978-1-62275-974-3 (6-pack)
1. Constitutional law — United States — Juvenile literature. I. Title.
KF4550.Z9W397 2015
342.73 — dc23

                                                                2014037268

Manufactured in the United States of America

Photo credits: Cover, interior pages background image © iStockphoto.com/oersin; p. 4 © AP Images; pp. 5, 6 National Archives; p. 7 © H. Armstrong Roberts/ClassicStock/The Image Works; p. 8 Bruce Yuanyue Bi/Lonely Planet Images/Getty Images; p. 9 Stock Montage/Archive Photos/Getty Images; p. 10 © North Wind Picture Archives; p. 11 The Bridgeman Art Library/Getty Images; p. 12 © World History Archive/TopFoto/The Image Works; p. 13 Universal History Archive/UIG/Bridgeman Images; p. 14 MPI/Archive Photos/Getty Images; p. 15 Kids.gov; p. 16 Steve Bronstein/The Image Bank/Getty Images; p. 17 Bloomberg/Getty Images; p. 18 Caroline Purser/Photographer's Choice/Getty Image; p. 19 Official White House Photo by Pete Souza; pp. 20, 21 Library of Congress Prints and Photographs Division Washington, D.C.; p. 22 Nationalaltas.gov/U.S. Department of the Interior; p. 23 Gary Tognoni/iStock/Thinkstock; p. 24 Aaron Haupt/Science Source/Getty Images; p. 25 Stock Montage/Archive Photos/Getty Images; p. 26 Ron Chapple/The Image Bank/Getty Images; p. 28 New York Public Library, USA/Bridgeman Images; p. 29 John Parrot/Stocktrek Images/Getty Images

CONTENTS

What Is the Constitution?

Laws are the rules made by a government. In the United States, there are three levels of government: local, state, and national. Local governments make laws for cities, towns, and counties. State governments make laws for a whole state. The national government makes laws for the whole country.

You can view the United States Constitution at the National Archives in Washington, D.C.

The Magna Carta, shown here, was signed by England's King John.

The U.S. Constitution is the most basic law of the United States government. All local, state, and national laws must agree with it.

The Constitution also established a federal system for the country. This means that the national government has certain powers and the states have other powers.

THINK ABOUT IT

The writers of the Constitution drew their ideas from many sources. One important one was England's Magna Carta. Signed in the year 1215, it guaranteed basic rights to English people.

BEFORE THE CONSTITUTION

The first constitution of the United States was called the Articles of Confederation. The document was written after the 13 North American colonies declared their independence from Great Britain. It went into effect in 1781.

The Articles of Confederation set up the government of the United States, but its shortcomings soon became apparent to the nation's leaders.

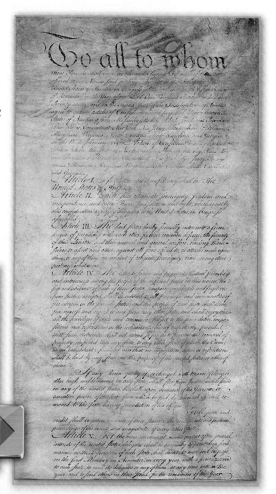

THINK ABOUT IT

Under the Articles of Confederation, Congress could not raise money through collecting taxes. It could only ask the states for money. Do you think states would be likely to give money if they did not have to?

The Articles of Confederation did not work well. It gave the United States a weak national government and strong state governments. Congress had no way to enforce its power and so could not make states follow the laws. After only a few years, the nation's leaders started talking about ways to improve the Articles of Confederation.

The men who wrote the Articles of Confederation were members of the Second Continental Congress. Members of the Congress also wrote the Declaration of Independence in 1776.

THE CONSTITUTIONAL CONVENTION

The Constitutional Convention met between May 25 and September 17, 1787, in Philadelphia, Pennsylvania. Every state except for Rhode Island sent delegates to the convention. The convention was called so that these delegates could talk about improving the way that the United States government worked.

The Constitution was written at Independence Hall in Philadelphia, which still stands today.

George Washington was chosen to lead the Constitutional Convention. Many other of the Founding Fathers were there as representatives of their states. These well-known representatives included Benjamin Franklin, Alexander Hamilton, and James Madison.

The delegates soon decided to discard the Articles of Confederation. They wanted a document that created a strong central government but that still gave the states some powers.

Alexander Hamilton represented New York at the Constitutional Convention.

DEBATE AND COMPROMISE

The delegates debated how to balance power between the states and the national government. They also debated two plans for how the states would be represented. Under the New Jersey Plan, each state would have the same number of representatives. This plan was better for small states.

LAND CLAIMS
OF THE
THIRTEEN ORIGINAL STATES
IN 1783.
New York claimed all the lands west of the Alleghany Mts. and North of the Ohio River belonging to the Six Nations.

This map shows what the United States looked like at the time of the Constitutional Convention.

James Madison wrote the Virginia Plan. He is known as "the Father of the Constitution."

Under the Virginia Plan, the number of representatives would be based on the population of each state. This plan was better for big states.

In the end, delegates compromised, and ideas from both plans are in the Constitution. Compromise means people with different ideas give up a little of what they want to make an agreement.

COMPARE AND CONTRAST

Each plan had different ideas about how states should be represented. Can you see how one plan favored big states and the other plan favored small states?

THE GREAT COMPROMISE

The delegates eventually agreed on the Great Compromise. The national legislature would have two houses. In the Senate, each state would have the same number of members. In the House of Representatives, representation would be based on each state's population.

Northern and Southern states then disagreed on whether slaves should be included in a state's population. Delegates from southern states thought

Connecticut delegates Oliver Ellsworth *(left)* and Roger Sherman *(right)* helped draw up the Great Compromise.

The TOBACCO-MANUFACTORY in different Branches.

Slaves were forced to work on large plantations in the Southern states.

that both free people and slaves should be counted in a state's population. Some delegates from northern states wanted to end slavery. Others said that if slavery were allowed, a state's representation should depend only on the free population.

Then the delegates finally reached another compromise. Representation for each state would be based on the number of free people and three-fifths of the number of slaves in the state.

THINK ABOUT IT

Why was it important for Southern states that slaves be counted in their populations?

BALANCING POWER

The writers of the Constitution wanted a strong central government. They did not want this government to take *too* much power, though. They decided to split the government's power among three equal branches: the legislative, executive, and judicial branches. Each branch has a different function. Splitting the government's power is called the separation of powers.

The Constitution states that each branch of government has some power over the others. This is

This painting shows the delegates signing the finished Constitution.

known as a system of checks and balances. Checks and balances make sure that the three branches of government share power, making sure that no one branch gets too powerful.

This chart shows the three branches of government and the duties of each one.

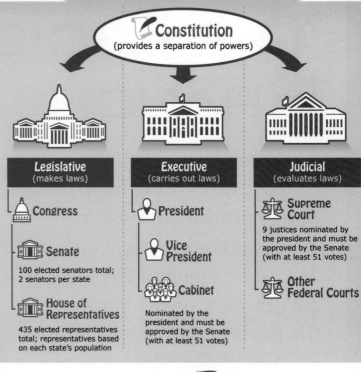

COMPARE AND CONTRAST

In the system of checks and balances, the legislative branch makes laws. The executive branch can reject these laws. The judicial branch can say these laws are wrong. Do you think that this system works well?

THE LEGISLATIVE BRANCH

The main body of the Constitution is made up of the **Preamble** and seven Articles. Each Article either describes a part of the government or explains how the government works.

Article One describes the legislative branch, known as

Article One of the Constitution describes the structure of the legislative branch of the government.

Congress meets in the building called the Capitol in Washington, D.C.

Congress. The Constitution gives Congress the power to write laws, raise taxes, borrow money, and declare war.

There are two houses of Congress. One is the Senate, which has two members from each state. The other is the House of Representatives. The number of representatives for each state is based on the state's population. Article One says who can become a senator or a representative and how long their terms are.

Actions by the legislative branch are checked by both the president and the Supreme Court.

THE EXECUTIVE BRANCH

Article Two of the Constitution describes the executive branch. The president is the leader of this branch. The president has many jobs, including being the head of the military, choosing whether to approve or veto (reject) laws passed by Congress, and appointing (choosing) people for important government jobs.

The president lives in the White House.

Here, President Barack Obama is meeting with Vice President Joe Biden in the Oval Office in the White House.

There are checks to the executive branch's powers. The Supreme Court can decide that the president's actions are not allowed by the Constitution. The Senate must approve the people whom the president appoints. Congress can override a president's veto if enough members in each chamber vote to do so.

COMPARE AND CONTRAST

Compare and contrast the checks and balances between the three branches of government. How do they encourage the branches to work together? How do they keep each branch from getting too much power?

THE JUDICIAL BRANCH

Article Three of the Constitution describes the judicial branch, which is the system of state and federal courts. Article Three states the kinds of cases that this court system handles.

The Supreme Court is the head of the judicial branch. The Supreme Court also explains the meaning of the laws in the Constitution. Justices can decide whether new or

In 1896 the Supreme Court ruled that laws keeping African Americans separate from whites were constitutional. This was called segregation.

In 1954, the Supreme Court overturned an earlier ruling and made segregation unconstitutional.

old laws agree with the Constitution or if they are unconstitutional. Unconstitutional laws are overturned.

The other two branches balance the judicial branch's powers. The president appoints justices to the Supreme Court, but the Senate must then approve justices. Once justices join the Supreme Court or another federal court they can stay until they decide to step down.

STATE AND FEDERAL GOVERNMENTS

Article Four of the Constitution describes how the states relate to each other. It says that states must respect the official acts and public records of the other states. It also says that each state's laws must treat citizens from other states the same as they do their own citizens. Article Four also describes how

This map shows the United States today.

new states can join the country.

Article Six made the Constitution the supreme law of the United States. It says that the Constitution and other federal laws have to be followed by every state, even if state laws on the same subject do not agree with federal laws. Article Four and Article Six helped form the stronger central government than its writers wanted to create.

THINK ABOUT IT

Under the Articles of Confederation, states did not have to respect other states' laws. Why would this situation cause problems between states?

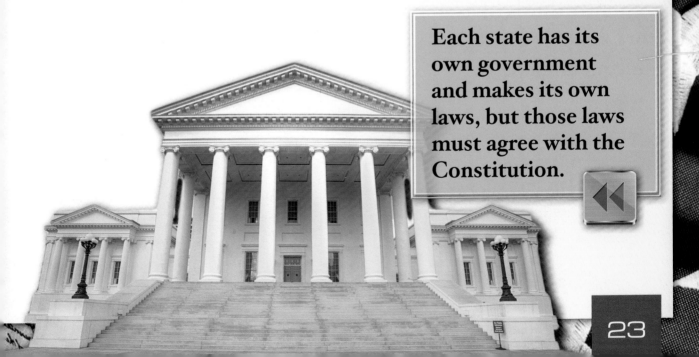

Each state has its own government and makes its own laws, but those laws must agree with the Constitution.

CHANGES TO THE CONSTITUTION

Article Five describes how the Constitution can be changed. Such a change is called an amendment.

It is not easy to change the Constitution. First an amendment has to be proposed. There are two ways that can happen.

Two-thirds of each house of Congress can agree on an amendment, or

VOCABULARY

An **amendment** is a change that is made to correct a mistake.

Drafting the Bill of Rights, shown here, was key to getting all of the states to ratify the Constitution.

two-thirds of the states can call for a Constitutional Convention to suggest an amendment.

After an amendment has been proposed, three-fourths of the states must approve it before it is added to the Constitution.

There have been only 27 amendments added to the Constitution. The first ten amendments are called the Bill of Rights. They guarantee citizens certain rights and place limits on the government. Other amendments include the Thirteenth Amendment, which ended slavery, and the Nineteenth Amendment, which gave women the right to vote.

The Nineteenth Amendment was added in 1920.

THE BILL OF RIGHTS

The amendments that make up the Bill of Rights were written in 1789 and added to the Constitution in 1791. The amendments protect the rights of individual citizens.

The First Amendment gives the right to free speech and a free press. It also gives people the right

The Bill of Rights defines the rights of a citizen on trial.

to protest and to practice religion freely. The Second Amendment is the right to bear arms, meaning the right to own weapons. The Third Amendment says that the government cannot make citizens house soldiers.

The Fourth Amendment says that the government must have a judge's permission to search property. The Fifth, Sixth, and Seventh Amendments explain the rights a citizen has in a trial. The Eighth Amendment protects citizens from cruel punishment.

The Ninth Amendment says that rights not stated in the Constitution belong to citizens. The Tenth Amendment says that powers not stated in the Constitution belong either to the states or to citizens.

THINK ABOUT IT

The Third Amendment was written because when the United States was a British colony, people could be forced to allow British soldiers to live in their homes. Can you see why people felt that having strangers in their houses went against their rights?

APPROVING THE CONSTITUTION

The Constitution was signed on September 17, 1787. Article Seven said that nine states needed to **ratify** the Constitution before it would go into effect.

Each state discussed whether or not to ratify the Constitution. Supporters of ratification were called Federalists because the Constitution set up a federal system of government. People against ratification were Anti-Federalists. Many Anti-Federalists did not want the Constitution ratified without a Bill of Rights.

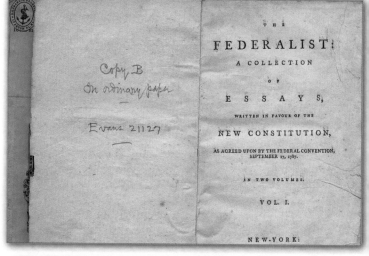

The Federalist Papers is a group of eighty-five essays written in support of ratifying the Constitution.

Five states quickly approved the Constitution. Other states took much longer to come to a decision.

The toughest debate was in New York. There, Alexander Hamilton and others wrote a series of essays to convince the New York government to ratify the Constitution. These essays are known as the Federalist Papers. New York approved the Constitution in 1788.

By 1790, all thirteen states had ratified the Constitution. With that important document as a guideline, the United States was well on its way to becoming a more united country.

Virginian George Washington played a key role in getting his state to support the Constitution. He became the first president of the United States in 1789.

GLOSSARY

Articles of Confederation The laws that governed the United States before the Constitution was created.

Bill of Rights The first ten amendments to the U.S. Constitution. They outline the basic rights guaranteed to the people of the United States.

compromise The settlement of a disagreement by each side giving up some of its demands.

Congress The main lawmaking body of the United States. It is made up of the Senate and the House of Representatives.

Constitutional Convention The meetings held in the summer of 1787 to create the Constitution.

debate To discuss an issue, often publicly, by presenting and considering different ideas about that issue.

delegates People sent with the power to vote or act for a group of people.

enforce To carry out a law.

executive Referring to the branch of government that carries out laws.

federal A form of government that balances power between a national government and state governments.

House of Representatives The part of the U.S. Congress in which the number of members a state has depends on the number of people living in that state.

judicial Referring to the branch of the government that contains the federal court system.

justices The nine judges on the Supreme Court are called justices. One is the chief justice. The others are associate justices.

legislative Referring to the branch of government that writes laws. This is Congress.

protest To display one's objection to something.

represented To have acted for a group of people.

right Something to which one has a just claim. In the United States, freedom of speech is a right.

Senate The part of the U.S. Congress in which every state has the same number of members (two).

slavery The condition in which a person is "owned" by another person.

veto The power of the president to stop a law passed by Congress.

For More Information

Books

Leavitt, Amie Jane. *The Constitution: Defender of Freedom*. Kennett Square, PA: Purple Toad Publishing, 2012.

Otfinoski, Steven. *The U.S. Constitution, Bill of Rights, and a New Nation*. Mankato, MN: Fact Finders, 2012.

Sobel, Syl. *The U.S. Constitution and You*. Hauppauge, NY: Barron's, 2012.

Sonneborn, Liz. *The United States Constitution*. Mankato, MN: Heinemann-Raintree, 2012.

Spier, Peter. *We the People*. New York, NY: Doubleday, 2014.

Websites

Because of the changing nature of Internet links, Rosen Publishing has developed an online list of websites related to the subject of this book. This site is updated regularly. Please use this link to access the list:

http://www.rosenlinks.com/LFO/Const

INDEX